CountryL D0566332

Spooky & Bright

CountryLiving

Spooky & Bright

101 HALLOWEEN IDEAS

From the Editors of
CountryLiving

HEARST BOOKS
New York

HEARST BOOKS
New York

An Imprint of Sterling Publishing
387 Park Avenue South
New York, NY 10016

ISBN: 978-1-61837-076-1

Design by: Alissa Faden

www.countryliving.com

Distributed in Canada by Sterling Publishing
C/o Canadian Manda Group, 165 Dufferin Street
Toronto, Ontario, Canada M6K 3H6

Distributed in Australia by Capricorn Link (Australia) Pty. Ltd.
P.O. Box 704, Windsor, NSW 2756 Australia

For information about custom editions, special sales, premium and corporate
purchases, please contact Sterling Special Sales Department at 800-805-5489
or specialsales@sterlingpub.com.

Manufactured in China

2 4 6 8 10 9 7 5 3 1

www.sterlingpublishing.com

Contents

See page 56 for how-to instructions.

Get in the Spirit!

I'M JUST GONNA PUT IT OUT THERE, at the risk of offending a large faction of yuletide fanatics: Halloween is, by far, my favorite holiday. The energy most people bring to trimming Christmas trees and wrapping gifts, I've already expended in October, decking the halls with faux cobwebs, rubber mice, and googly eyes galore.

Yes, I've lolled away untold hours curating curious little mise-en-scènes involving axes and tree stumps and plastic severed hands. An inventory of my past costumes includes a Miller beer can, fashioned from hula hoops and gold lamé, and a getup inspired by Tippi Hedren's character in *The Birds* (picture a sharp 1960s suit and a prim platinum wig wired with fake ravens). Did I mention that I'm 40-something, not four years old?

All of which is a long way of saying that you can count on *Country Living* to be completely obsessive about the most exciting night of the entire year. You'll find the proof on the following pages, packed with ingenious decorating tricks and sweet home-baked treats.

So fire up your glue gun, roll out the fondant, and meet me on the dark side!

Happy Halloween!

—Sarah Gray Miller
EDITOR-IN-CHIEF, *Country Living*

See page 26 for how-to instructions.

chapter one

Wicked-Smart Pumpkins

JACK-O'-LANTERNS—it wouldn't be Halloween without them. Every October, our porches, windows, and stoops come alive with tricked-out gourds glowing in the cool, dark night. Typically these pumpkins sport triangle eyes and crooked, snaggle-toothed grins. But we've packed this chapter with an array of spirited alternatives from skeletal arms reaching beyond the grave to ominous haunted houses to innovative designs drawn from nature.

You'll also find loads of creative "no carve" options that allow you to skip the knife altogether. These painted ravens, trees, insects, and spiderwebs capture Halloween themes for both indoor and outdoor display. Looking for simple, more graphic motifs? We've got you covered with gourds featuring bold stripes, chic chevron patterns, and beautiful faux-bois prints.

1

BECKON GUESTS WITH
these skeletal arms reaching from beyond the grave.

✤ **Step 1:** Select a pair of pumpkins to form each arm-hand combination. Determine which gourd will serve as the arm (usually the taller one) and trim its stem so that the other pumpkin can rest securely on top. Carve a hole in the bottom of each, scoop out the pulp, and set aside the cut bases.

✤ **Step 2:** Resize the skeletal templates on page 135 on a copier, scaling them to fit your pumpkins.

✤ **Step 3:** Cut out the templates and affix the arm template to the bottom pumpkin with masking tape. With a felt-tip pen, trace the design onto the pumpkin. Repeat the process on the other pumpkin with the hand template.

✤ **Step 4:** Remove the templates, then carefully carve along the drawn lines with an X-Acto knife. Affix a battery-operated votive candle to the base of each pumpkin with adhesive putty, reassemble each pumpkin and base, and then stack the pumpkins. Repeat the process with additional pairs of pumpkins to create a graveyard effect.

2

TAKE YOUR CREATIVE CUE from the great outdoors. This pumpkin's pattern—scored into the surface with a linoleum cutter—was modeled after woodgrain. For how-to tips, see page 130.

3

INSPIRATION IS EVERYWHERE. This pumpkin's simple design was patterned after fall leaves. For how-to tips, see page 130.

4

PUT A CHEEKY spin on the very word *jack-o'-lantern* with these glowing silhouettes of old-fashioned lamps.

+ **Step 1:** Cut your pumpkin around the stem, remove the top, and scoop out the pulp. (Or, to avoid visible cut lines, carve a hole out of the bottom of the pumpkin and remove the pulp that way.)

+ **Step 2:** Resize the lantern template on page 136 on a copier, scaling the image to fit your pumpkin. Download the additional lantern templates at countryliving.com/Oct-templates.

+ **Step 3:** Cut out the template and center it on the pumpkin, affixing it with masking tape. Outline the shape onto the pumpkin with a felt-tip pen.

+ **Step 4:** With the template still affixed to the pumpkin, use an awl to punch through the asterisks marked at the top of the lantern.

+ **Step 5:** Remove the template and carve out the pane(s) of the lantern, following the lines you drew.

+ **Step 6:** Carefully fill in the design with a fine-tip brush and black flat acrylic craft paint and let dry.

+ **Step 7:** Light the pumpkin with a 2- by 3-inch battery-operated votive candle. If you've removed the pumpkin's top, fit it back into place.

5

FOR A TRULY SMASHING PUMPKIN, consider découpage. It delivers more polish than a traditional carved pumpkin and more staying power.

✦ **Step 1:** Choose your favorite drawings from books, magazines, or the Internet (for this medium-size Funkin* we used approximately 120 small images from *Pictorial Webster's*, published by Chronicle Books), then photocopy them onto off-white cover stock paper.

✦ **Step 2:** Carefully tear out each photocopied image, leaving about half an inch of space around it. (The rough edges will give your finished product a layered, textured feel.)

✦ **Step 3:** Using the découpage technique detailed on page 130, cover an entire pumpkin with the images, overlapping their edges as you work.

*Funkins are hollow foam orbs that look like real pumpkins and can be carved like them. In addition to being lightweight, they allow you to preserve your handiwork for future Halloweens.

GO OUT ON A LIMB with this darling mama-and-baby duo.

✛ **Step 1:** Resize the templates on pages 137 on a copier, scaling the images to fit one large and one small pumpkin.

✛ **Step 2:** Cut out the templates and, using a felt-tip pen, trace the outlines onto pumpkins (as shown). Use a fine-tip brush to fill in the outlines with black flat acrylic paint. To detail additional features—such as eyes and wings—in relief, wait until the paint is dry to the touch, about five minutes, and scrape paint away with a bamboo skewer.

✛ **Step 3:** For the nest, select a third pumpkin that's large enough to hold the baby pumpkin. Using this photo as a guide, paint branches along the pumpkin's bottom half. Let the paint dry for one hour, then carefully cut the pumpkin along the tops of the branches with a sharp knife. Scoop out the pumpkin, fill it with moss, and tuck the baby pumpkin inside.

⟨7⟩

LET YOUR PUMPKINS DO THE TALKING. Here, a trio of festive pumpkins carved with letters and set on a diving platform spell out a seasonal greeting for visitors.

⟨8⟩

BUILD A QUAINT VILLAGE
with a passel of pumpkins.

+ **Step 1:** Carve a hole in the bottom of each pumpkin, scoop out the pulp, and set aside the cut base.

+ **Step 2:** Resize the house template on page 136 on a copier, scaling the image to fit your pumpkin. Download additional house templates at country living.com/oct-templates.

+ **Step 3:** Cut out the templates and affix them to the pumpkins with masking tape. Trace the designs onto the pumpkins with a felt-tip pen.

+ **Step 4:** Remove the templates, then carefully carve along the drawn lines of the houses' windows with an X-Acto knife. Fill in the designs using a fine-tip brush and black flat acrylic paint; let dry. Affix a battery-operated votive candle to the base of each pumpkin with adhesive putty, and reassemble each pumpkin and base.

9

SPIN A STORY. Feature Edgar Allan Poe's ominous poem "The Raven" by spelling out a few lines with stick-on letters (check out Etsy.com). Affix them in a spiral pattern, starting at the top. To give the dark words even more presence, first use a foam brush to cover your pumpkin with two coats of white or pale-gray acrylic paint, allowing 30 minutes of drying time per coat. For the accompanying raven, simply apply a decal to a second pumpkin.

⇒ 10 ⇐

ACHIEVE AN ENCHANTING EFFECT

by scoring the skin of a pumpkin with curlicues or other motifs using linoleum cutting tools. For how-to tips, see page 130.

⊶❦11❦⊷

SET YOUR HEARTH ABLAZE with these rip-roaring flames.

✢ **Step 1:** Begin by experimenting with the placement of the pumpkins in your fireplace. Once you're satisfied with the arrangement, trim any stems that interfere with the arrangement's stability, then determine how many flames each gourd should get. (Use this photo as a guide.) Make a sketch showing where each pumpkin goes (you'll need to refer to it later) and dismantle the arrangement.

✢ **Step 2:** Carve a hole in the bottom of each pumpkin, scoop out the pulp, and set aside the cut base.

✢ **Step 3:** Use the flame templates on page 134 (if necessary, resize the templates on a photocopier to fit your pumpkins), or draw flames freehand.

✢ **Step 4:** Cut out the templates and affix them to the pumpkins with masking tape. Trace the designs onto the pumpkins with a felt-tip pen.

✢ **Step 5:** Remove the templates, then carefully carve along the drawn lines with an X-Acto knife. Affix a battery-operated votive candle in the base of each pumpkin with adhesive putty, and reassemble each pumpkin and base. Using the sketch as a guide, re-create your arrangement.

(For projects 12 to 14, see the photo on page 8.)

⊶ 12 ⊷

MAKE A CREEPY BEETLE look chic
with a stark black-and-white palette.

✦ **Step 1:** Brush the entire pumpkin with a coat of white
flat acrylic craft paint and let dry for 20 minutes.

✦ **Step 2:** Download the beetle template at
countryliving.com/oct-templates. Resize the
template on a copier, scaling the image to fit your
pumpkin. Cut out the template and affix it to the
pumpkin with stencil adhesive.

✦ **Step 3:** Paint the beetle within the stencil using three
coats of black flat acrylic craft paint. Let the paint
dry for 30 minutes and remove the stencil.

⊶ 13 ⊷

GIVE A SPOOKY SPIDERWEB
added dimension by featuring it on
a white pumpkin.

✦ **Step 1:** Brush the entire pumpkin with a coat of white
flat acrylic craft paint and let dry for 20 minutes.

✦ **Step 2:** Using a black fine-tip paint pen, draw a circle
around the top of the pumpkin, about two inches
from the stem. Keep drawing a continuous line,

spiraling around the perimeter of the pumpkin, as shown, until you reach the base.

+ **Step 3:** Draw vertical lines in the pumpkin's crevices, starting from the circle near the stem and going to the bottom of the pumpkin.

+ **Step 4:** Let the paint dry for 30 minutes, then place one or two plastic spiders on the "web."

⊷ 14 ⊶

TURN THE EXPECTED INTO THE UNEXPECTED: Choose this bold, graphic wood-grain pattern.

+ **Step 1:** Brush the entire pumpkin with a coat of white flat acrylic craft paint and let dry for 20 minutes.

+ **Step 2:** Mix a small amount of clear glaze with black flat acrylic craft paint.

+ **Step 3:** Drawing freehand with a fine-tip brush and the photo as a guide, begin painting several irregular circles around the pumpkin, as shown, spacing them at varying heights.

+ **Step 4:** To complete the pattern, fill the rest of the pumpkin's surface with curving lines. Let the paint dry for 30 minutes.

⟶ 15 ⟵

SHOOT FOR THE MOON with this celestial creation, meant to mimic the look of that classic childhood toy, the Lite-Brite.

✛ **Step 1:** Cut your pumpkin around the stem, remove the top, and scoop out the pulp. (Or to avoid visible cut lines, carve a hole out of the bottom of the pumpkin and remove the pulp that way.)

✛ **Step 2:** Using a round object such as a plate for a guide, lightly score the curves of the moon onto your pumpkin.

✛ **Step 3:** With an awl, punch the outline of the design through the pumpkin's flesh.

✛ **Step 4:** Fit each hole with a bulb from a set of battery-powered string lights.

✛ **Step 5:** Fit the top (or bottom) of the pumpkin back into place.

⚔ 16 ⚔

CREATE THESE NIFTY DESIGNS using only acrylic paint and painter's tape.

⊹ For a two-tone dipped look, bisect a pumpkin with a strip of tape (angle the tape for a diagonal effect). Use a foam brush to cover one section of your pumpkin with two coats of acrylic paint, allowing 30 minutes of drying time per coat. Remove the tape and discard. Stop there, or repeat the steps to add another color to your pumpkin.

⊹ To form chevron stripes—whether two or tons— link short strips of tape to make the zigzag patterns, using this photo as a guide. Use a foam brush to cover your pumpkin with two coats of acrylic paint, allowing 30 minutes of drying time per coat. Remove the tape and discard. Clean up the edges with a cotton swab if necessary. If you'd like the second color to be differ-ent than natural pumpkin orange, fill in using a small paintbrush and contrasting acrylic paint, as we did for the black-and-white pumpkin.

⚔ 17 ⚔

TIP: Orange isn't the only option when it comes to pumpkins. Choose ghostly white Lumina pumpkins or large, warty Blue Hubbard gourds to round out your Halloween display. Visit your local pumpkin patch or farmstand for other suitably spooky varieties.

18

THE SECRET to these moth-adorned marvels? Weather-resistant vinyl decals (for similar, check out Etsy.com). Show them to their best advantage on white pumpkins. Use a foam brush to cover each pumpkin with two coats of white acrylic paint, allowing 30 minutes of drying time per coat, then apply decals.

⊶ 19 ⊶

PART COBWEB, part creeping vine, the effect of black lace on painted pumpkins is thoroughly macabre. Begin by painting pumpkins (we opted for a pale green-blue color). Once they're dry, use this photo as a guide to cut out pieces of lace; brush matte Mod Podge onto the back of the lace, and adhere the lace to your pumpkins. Finish by sealing each with a topcoat of Mod Podge.

✦ 20 ✦

TO MAKE THIS ENCHANTING TREE
start with a sturdy bookcase.

✦ **Step 1:** Begin by experimenting with the placement of pumpkins on your shelves. Your tree should gradually widen toward the top, with multiple smaller gourds on higher shelves. Also, if there's a good deal of space between two shelves, you may need to stack pumpkins to fill it (as we did on the bottom shelf here). In that case, trim any stems that interfere with stacking stability. (Concerned about the heft of pumpkins on a particular shelf? Opt for lightweight, faux Funkins.)

✦ **Step 2:** Using this photo as a guide, draw the outline of a tree onto the pumpkins with a felt-tip pen. Start at the bottom and branch out as you move up. (You may need to use a stepladder to reach upper shelves.)

✦ **Step 3:** Working one shelf at a time, remove the pumpkins and fill in your outlines with a fine-tip brush and two coats of black flat acrylic paint, allowing 15 minutes of drying time between coats. Finally, replace the pumpkins in your bookcase.

⇛ 21 ⇚

PERCH A FEW jack-o'-lanterns and a flock of
faux black crows in a bare tree. If your tree's limbs
aren't sturdy enough to support real pumpkins, consider
lightweight, faux Funkins.

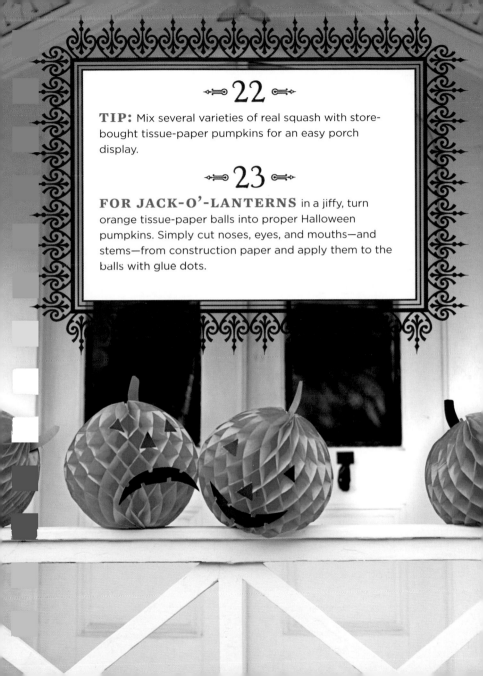

⇒ 22 ⇐

TIP: Mix several varieties of real squash with store-bought tissue-paper pumpkins for an easy porch display.

⇒ 23 ⇐

FOR JACK-O'-LANTERNS in a jiffy, turn orange tissue-paper balls into proper Halloween pumpkins. Simply cut noses, eyes, and mouths—and stems—from construction paper and apply them to the balls with glue dots.

24

SCORE YOUR PUMPKIN (here, a "Blue Hubbard") with motifs inspired by thorny branches using linoleum cutters. For how-to tips, see page 130.

25

CHOOSE THE BEST gourd for your pattern: This "Cinderella" pumpkin has deep reddish-orange skin and bright orange flesh, dramatically evoking the fabric beneath it. For how-to tips, see page 130.

⇐ 26 ⇒

CREATE AN AVIAN-THEMED tabletop tableau. To make this pumpkin, download the templates for the bird and feather at countryliving.com/oct-templates. Resize the templates on a copier, scaling the images to fit your pumpkins, then trace the outlines onto the pumpkins. Use a fine-tip brush to fill in the outlines with black flat acrylic paint. Let dry for one hour. Set both pumpkins under cloches, with one pumpkin resting on a bed of moss. Add a bird painting, a spotted egg (or eggshells), more moss, and a nest to complete the scene.

⇐ 27 ⇒

TIP: To make candles last longer, freeze them for two hours before placing them in votives or pumpkins. The chilled wax will slow the burning.

WHINCHAT
PLATE 9.

See page 81 for how-to instructions.

chapter two

Haunt Your House

DELICATE COBWEBS, EBONY RAVENS, FLICKERING LIGHTS— the visual harbingers of Halloween can be as elegant as they are eerie. Get ready to fall under the spell of our decorating ideas, guaranteed to make your guests shiver with delight.

The following pages boast DIY projects so easy it's scary: a wreath made from rubber eyeballs, for example, and a witch's hat topping a family portrait. Learn how to imbue your home with a certain sinister sophistication, via artfully draped sheets, a vase of gnarled branches, or cheesecloth cobwebs. And employ our clever entertaining tricks to host a monstrously memorable bash.

Of course, we didn't stop at the sights of the season; you'll also discover tips for putting together a spine-tingling soundtrack of creaks, moans, and groans. With spirited advice like this, you're sure to have a blast setting the mood for mischief!

28

SERVE UP A DARING DISPLAY with this novel idea for old plates.

✢ **Step 1:** Use the bird templates on page 138 (or download additional birds at countryliving.com/oct-templates). Resize the templates on a copier, scaling the images to fit your plates. Trace their outlines onto plates with a pencil.

✢ **Step 2:** Use a fine-tip brush to fill in the outlines with black flat acrylic paint. To detail additional features—such as eyes and wings—in relief, wait until the paint is dry to the touch, about five minutes, and scrape paint away with a bamboo skewer. Let these plates, which are for decoration only, dry for one hour before mounting them using plate hangers.

29

TIP: Cast an eerie glow over your guests by putting green lightbulbs in your lamps.

30

YOU WON'T BE ABLE TO take your eyes off this wreath. To create it, you'll need about eight dozen glow-in-the-dark rubber eyeballs and a 12-inch-foam wreath form. Wrap the form in black crepe-paper streamers and secure them with straight pins. Poke a hole in the back of one eyeball with the sharp end of a flatheaded pin; then insert the pin's flat end into the hole. Using a thimble to protect your finger, press the pin halfway in. Push the sharp end of the pin into the foam. Repeat until the wreath is full and hang as desired.

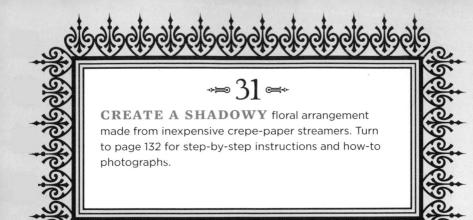

⊷ 31 ⊷

CREATE A SHADOWY floral arrangement
made from inexpensive crepe-paper streamers. Turn
to page 132 for step-by-step instructions and how-to
photographs.

32

TAKE A WREATH—a traditional harbinger of goodwill—to the dark side. Turn to page 131 for step-by-step instructions and how-to photographs.

⊷ 33 ⊶

GIVE NEW MEANING to the term *bird-watching* with mischievous crow stickers. Creating these avian silhouettes is easy. Carefully copy, resize, then trace the templates on page 138 onto static-cling window decal sheets. Cut out the bird shapes, press them onto windowpanes, and smooth out any air bubbles.

⊶ 34 ⊷

TURN AN INNOCUOUS SOFA into a horror-show set piece by draping it with tattered cheesecloth.

⊶ 35 ⊷

ADD A JOLT of humor to a solemn portrait by topping the subject's head with a construction-paper witch's hat.

⊶ 36 ⊷

AFFIX CUTOUT BATS to the wall, door, and elsewhere with double-sided tape.

⊶ 37 ⊷

TIP: Record a soundtrack of creepy cackles, creaks, howls, and moans to spook trick-or-treaters or party guests. Ordinary household items can be used to create spine-chilling sound effects. Leather-soled shoes, for example, can be knocked together to mimic the sound of footsteps pacing the floor.

➤ 38 ⬅

FOR A GROWN-UP HALLOWEEN, turn fright night into an elegantly eerie affair with sophisticated accessories such as black and white dishes embellished with skull images and a resin bird perched on a cake stand.

➤ 39 ⬅

CREATE A GOTHIC GLOW by using black goblets as candleholders.

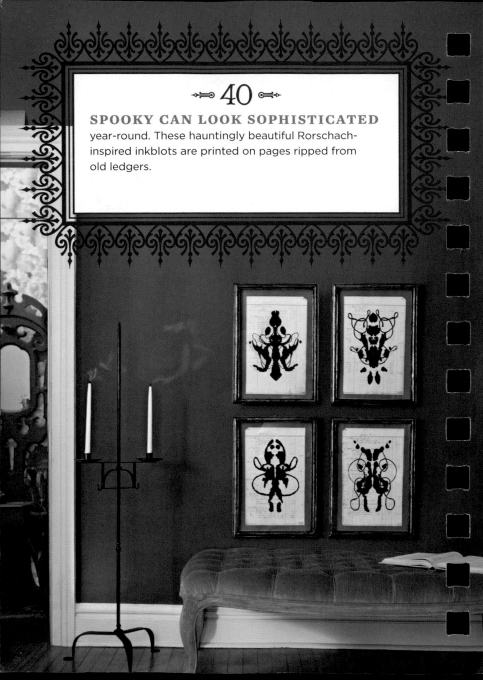

40

SPOOKY CAN LOOK SOPHISTICATED

year-round. These hauntingly beautiful Rorschach-inspired inkblots are printed on pages ripped from old ledgers.

41

TRANSFORM AN ORDINARY PEN into a severed finger. Pinch off a piece of Model Magic that's slightly smaller than a golf ball. Working on a clean surface, use your hands to roll and flatten the claylike material into a strip approximately 1"W x 5"L. Wrap it around a ballpoint pen, leaving the nib exposed. Roll the wrapped pen on your work surface to smooth, then use your hands and a toothpick to shape knuckles and wrinkles. Finish by inserting a fake black fingernail into the clay over the nib, ensuring that the nib extends far enough to allow for writing. Let dry for one day before using.

⊷ 42 ⊷

ORANGE PAPER LANTERNS take an ominous turn with a little help from plain tissue paper. Download the bird template at countryliving.com/oct-templates and resize on a copier to fit your lanterns. Cut out, and then trace the outline onto black tissue paper. Cut out the shape; repeat as desired. Run a glue stick along the back of each shape before carefully affixing it to a lantern. You can suspend the lanterns over pendant bulbs, or just string them up empty, as we did—the more the scarier.

⊷ 43 ⊷

DON'T FORGET TO costume *everyone*—even folks in paintings and photos. Black construction paper, scissors, and lower-tack artists' tape were all it took to ready the blushing bride in the portrait on page 6 for a masquerade ball. Just resist the urge to disguise priceless artwork that's not protected by glass.

44

AN ANTIQUE BIRDCAGE—OR TWO, as seen here—can host any seasonal display, but decorated with faux black crows it's especially perfect for Halloween.

45

LEAVE NO CORNER UNSPOOKED— drape cheesecloth "cobwebs" over chairs, lamps, and doors throughout the house.

46

DARE GUESTS TO CLEAN UP with these creepy critter soaps. You'll need soap molds, extra-clear soap base, and plastic bug toys. Following package instructions and using a candy thermometer, melt the soap base in a large pot on the stove until it reaches 140°F. Place one plastic bug belly-up in each mold. Slowly pour the melted soap into the molds until it reaches the very top. Wait for bubbles to rise, then use a knife to scrape them off. Let the molds sit on a flat surface overnight, then remove the soaps, and you're ready to lather up.

47

TURN ORDINARY GLASS vases into display cases for raven silhouettes perched inside. Resize the templates on page 139 on a copier, scaling the images to fit your vases, and print them onto card stock. Using a utility knife, cut out each silhouette and lightly score along its dotted lines, then fold the card stock back along the scores you just made. (If you're making the tall raven, cut a bamboo skewer to the size indicated on the template and tape it to the card stock as directed.) Next, apply craft glue to the bottom tab, as indicated on the stencil, and fold closed to form a triangular base. Place a few small stones or coins inside the base to weight it down, if necessary.

48

SCARE UP a mini ghost town. Inspired by a post on fellowfellow.com, this project uses an image of any building—be it your home, or a ghoulish landmark like the Bates Motel—to transform a standard glass votive holder. Begin by copying the image you've chosen onto plain paper or card stock (resizing if necessary, so the building is wide enough to wrap around your votive holder). Using an X-Acto knife, cut around the roofline and any treetops; also cut out windows where glass panes would be. Wrap the image around your votive holder, securing the ends with clear tape. Lastly, pop a battery-operated candle into the holder and flick on the spectral flames.

49

TURN SMALL GOURDS into votive candle-holders by cutting off the stem and carving out enough pulp to make room for a votive candle.

50

TRANSFORM IMAGES of loved ones into a ghostly display.

+ **Step 1:** Make a black-and-white copy of a portrait on printer paper and cut out.

+ **Step 2:** To "age" the picture, lightly brush it with a sponge dipped in a solution of a few drops of black craft paint mixed with water. Let the paper dry for 20 minutes.

+ **Step 3:** Cut a piece of card stock the same size as the photocopied portrait, glue it to the photocopy's back with a glue stick, and let dry. With an X-Acto knife, cut out the eyes of the pictures' subject(s), piercing through the card stock and creating holes about ¼ inch in diameter.

+ **Step 4:** Open the frame's back, remove the glass, then fit the photo inside.

+ **Step 5:** Insert red mini LED Christmas lights through the back of the eyeholes. Plug in the lights, then replace the frame's backing—securing it with tape if necessary—and drape with fake cobwebs.

❧ 51 ❧

LURE VISITORS TO YOUR DOOR
with a spiderweb mat.

✦ **Step 1:** Purchase an indoor/outdoor needle-punch carpet. To turn it into a circle, mark the rug's center point with a white-colored pencil. Measure and mark the distance from the center point to a spot about half an inch from the rug's edge. Cut a piece of string to that length. Tie one end of the string to the pencil and secure the other end of the string to the rug's center point with a tack. Pull the string taut and draw a large circle onto the rug, then remove the string. Cut out the circle, just inside the white pencil mark, with sharp scissors.

✦ **Step 2:** Using a yardstick, evenly space and draw eight intersecting lines that cross the rug from edge to edge. Between those lines, draw arches around the mat, using the photo here as a guide.

✦ **Step 3:** Coat the rug with a clear finishing spray to protect your web from trick-or-treating feet.

❧ 52 ❧

IMBUE EVERY ROOM of the house with the spirit of Halloween. Here, a faux spiderweb stretches from the window to a stack of magazines and a half-eaten apple on a nightstand.

53

GIVE PAPER DOLLS a poisonous twist. Here, the classic schoolgirl pastime graduates from cute craft to gothic decor.

✢ **Step 1:** Cut a 5″W x 18″L strip from a 12″W x 18″L sheet of construction paper. Measure in three inches from one of the five-inch ends and mark the spot. From there, measure in three inches more and mark; repeat three more times.

✢ **Step 2:** Fold the paper at the first mark. Then flip the paper over and fold again at the next mark. Keep flipping and folding the paper, making an accordion.

✢ **Step 3:** Trace the spider template on page 140 and cut as directed. (This template doubles as a cake stencil!)

✢ **Step 4:** Center the template atop the folded paper, and trace around the shape with a pencil.

✢ **Step 5:** Carefully cut out the shape, going through all the layers of folded paper, and unfold to reveal. To create a longer row, repeat the steps and adhere the garlands together with tacky glue.

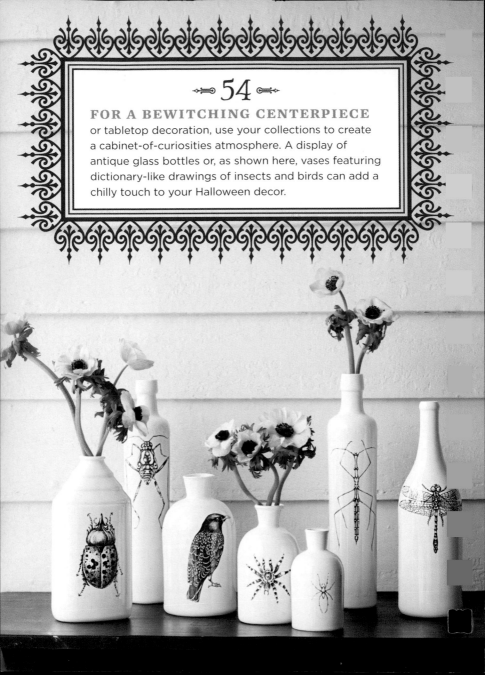

⟿ 54 ⟿

FOR A BEWITCHING CENTERPIECE
or tabletop decoration, use your collections to create
a cabinet-of-curiosities atmosphere. A display of
antique glass bottles or, as shown here, vases featuring
dictionary-like drawings of insects and birds can add a
chilly touch to your Halloween decor.

⟶ 55 ⟵

CRAFT HAUNTING TERRARIUMS out of empty pickle, jelly, and other glass jars. First, wash each container and dry thoroughly. Choose a sturdy twig that's slightly shorter and narrower than the jar and hot-glue it to the inside of the lid, so that the twig sticks straight up. Then hot-glue plastic bugs to the wood—making sure the bugs fit inside the glass when you seal the terrarium. Next, spray-paint everything but the jar—twig, bugs, lid—white or black. Once the piece has dried, hot-glue green floral moss around the base of the twig. Carefully place the jar upside down over the lid and screw it on. To make the crow version shown, follow the instructions above, but hot-glue a fake bird to the twig *after* you spray-paint.

⇥ 56 ⇤

CREATE A HOST of friendly ghosts. These spirited little cheesecloth specters are a cinch to make. Turn to page 133 for step-by-step instructions and photographs.

⬤ 60 ⬤

WELCOME TRICK-OR-TREATERS

in hair-raising style by embellishing your front door
with a flock of felt bats. Using the template on page
134, resize the image on a copier if desired, and cut as
directed. (This home features bats in different sizes.)
Fold a sheet of stiffened felt in half. Match up the
template's straight edge with the fold and outline the
half-bat shape onto the felt with chalk. Keeping the
material folded, cut just inside the chalk lines. Unfold
to reveal a full bat silhouette. Affix to exterior surfaces
with duct tape.

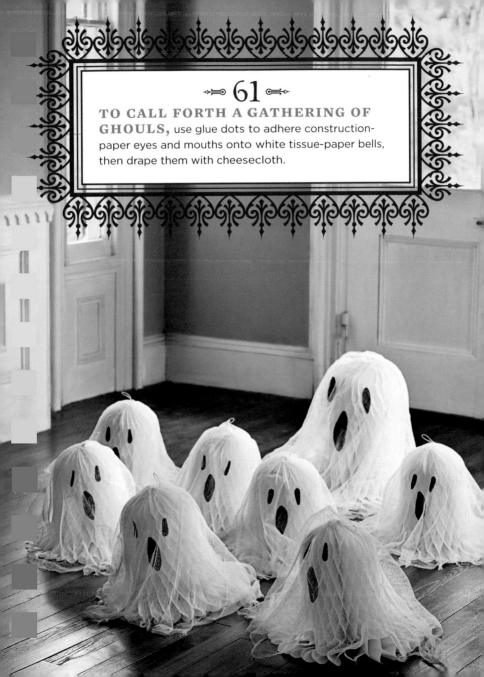

→ 61 ↔

TO CALL FORTH A GATHERING OF GHOULS, use glue dots to adhere construction-paper eyes and mouths onto white tissue-paper bells, then drape them with cheesecloth.

⟻ 62 ⟼

STOP DINNER GUESTS dead in their tracks with a custom-stamped tablecloth. To make your own talon stamp, use this photo as a guide and draw a crow's footprint or download our template at countryliving. com/oct-templates. Then, use it as a guide to carve a synthetic printing block (find them as well as carving tools at art supply stores). Press the block onto a fabric-friendly ink pad and stamp a wandering trail.

63

DRAW ATTENTION to the sculptural shape of squash by stacking two small specimens beneath a cloche. Trim the stem of the bottom squash so the other can rest securely on top.

⇒ 64 ⇐

GREET GUESTS with a welcoming display of decorative gourds. Layered with greenery, the gourds can create a lush look even in the confined space of a window box.

⇒ 65 ⇐

TIP: for an understated seasonal touch, line your front steps with a mixed—and uncarved—array of gourds including white, yellow, and orange examples.

⇒ 66 ⇐

CAST A FEW DARK SHADOWS with the glamorous candles shown on page 42. Cut a length of lace, lay it on a paper plate, and brush on nontoxic, nonflammable black tempera paint. Roll a pillar, taper, or votive across the trim to pick up the pattern. Don't worry if the transfer is imperfect—a slightly decayed appearance ups the elegance. Then, let the paint dry for at least an hour before lighting the candle.

SOMBER ILLUSTRATIONS on simple candleholders illuminate a night of magic.

✦ **Step 1:** Measure the height and circumference of the glass candleholder you want to transform.

✦ **Step 2:** Scan or download a copyright-free black-and-white illustration (we used antique drawings from *The Clip Art Book,* published by Gramercy). Using Adobe Photoshop or a similar photo-editing program, adjust the image's size and orientation to fit your vessel's measurements (it may help to print a sample first).

✦ **Step 3:** Once the image is the correct size, load your printer with white vellum and print the image. Gently set it on a flat surface for a few minutes to allow the ink to dry.

✦ **Step 4:** Trim the vellum so it measures exactly as tall as your candleholder and half an inch wider than its circumference.

✦ **Step 5:** Wrap the vellum around the candleholder and secure the overlapping ends with double-sided tape.

⊸ 68 ⊶

GIVE YOUR HOME-SWEET-HOME a frightfully decrepit look by draping chairs and sofas with white sheets.

⊸ 69 ⊶

HANG CHEESECLOTH across a mirror, framed piece of art, or lamp.

⊸ 70 ⊶

INSTEAD OF CANDLES, secure stark, curly willow branches in candlesticks with museum wax.

⊸ 71 ⊶

ARRANGE CANDLES of different heights across the mantel for a dramatic, glowing effect.

⊸ 72 ⊶

PUT A DARK SPIN on a staple of entertaining—the candelabra—by using ebony tapers.

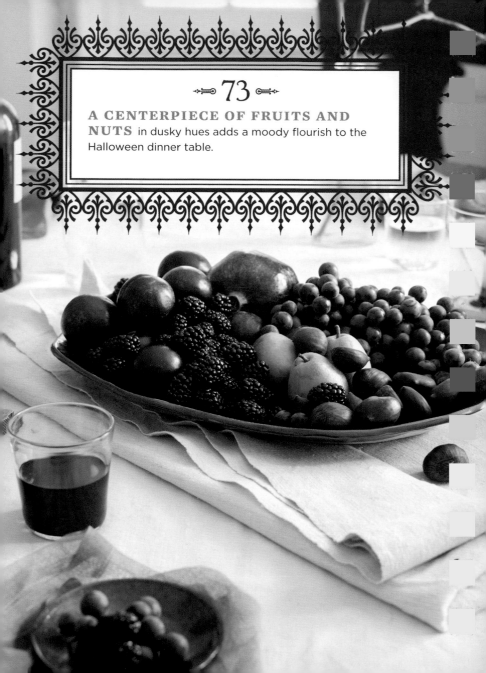

⊶ 73 ⊷

A CENTERPIECE OF FRUITS AND NUTS in dusky hues adds a moody flourish to the Halloween dinner table.

—◦ **74** ◦—

KEEP UP GHOSTLY APPEARANCES

with this witty reflection. Draw a figure on the back of
a sheet of frosted window film. Cut out the silhouette,
as well as its eyes and mouth, with an X-Acto knife.
Apply the film to a mirror, smoothing it as you go.

See page 127 for how-to instructions.

chapter three

Devilishly Delicious Treats

SURE, HALLOWEEN MAY BE THE ULTIMATE FRIGHT NIGHT, but the holiday also has a sweet side—and we're not just talking trick-or-treat candy. When else do baked goods take on such a variety of forms, from pumpkins to mice to full-fledged graveyards.

We've brewed up mad-genius ideas for decorating cakes, cupcakes, and cookies. There are playful nods to such hallowed Halloween symbols as the black cat, the spider, witches, and bats—as well as more outrageous desserts, like a chocolate-frosted X-ray with a gleaming sugar heart. And it wouldn't be October without candied apples, or caramel ones.

Of course, this chapter is chock-full of time-honored recipes, plus methods for making rich glazes, irresistible icings, and fondant figures. Is your mouth watering yet? Turn the page and sink your teeth into some seriously tasty inspiration.

➤ 75 ➤

DRESS UP HOMEMADE or store-bought cupcakes with this simple trick. Microwave fondant* icing for 8 to 10 seconds, then roll it out to a ¼-inch thickness. Using a cookie cutter or a glass, cut fondant frosting into circles and leave out overnight to stiffen. Paint a clean rubber stamp with black food coloring and gently press the image onto the circles of fondant. (We've used a stamp featuring a silhouette of a witch, but other images—cats, bats, crescent moons, for example—would work well, too.) If needed, fill in any bare spots on the silhouette with a small paintbrush dipped in the black food coloring. Just before serving, place the fondant circles on top of cupcakes with buttercream frosting.

➤ 76 ➤

TURN SUGAR COOKIES into "candy corn" cookies. To make this treat, knead extra flour and orange food coloring into refrigerated sugar-cookie dough (homemade or store-bought). Using a triangle-shaped cutter, cut out the cookies, bake according to package directions, and let cool. Dip the wide base of each cookie into melted dark chocolate, then dip the tip of each cookie into melted white chocolate. Set the cookies on a parchment-lined baking pan and chill in the freezer for 5 minutes.

*Fondant is available, in a variety of colors, at craft stores like Michaels and Jo-Ann.

⊷ 77 ⊶

GO BATTY with this fearsome flock.

✛ **Step 1:** Measure the height and width of your cake (this one's composed of two layers, held together by buttercream frosting in the middle). Next, double the height and then add the width plus one extra inch to determine the diameter to which you should roll out your fondant (you'll get one big number). Note: A 24-ounce package of fondant will be enough to cover an 8-inch two-layer cake. For larger cakes, add 6 more ounces for each 2-inch increase in cake's diameter.

✛ **Step 2:** Microwave the fondant for 8 to 10 seconds, then roll it out to ¼-inch thickness. Center and drape the rolled-out fondant over the cake. Begin molding it to the sides, loosening any folds by gently lifting and tucking the fondant back down. Smooth with your hands. Trim away any excess from the bottom with a pizza cutter.

✛ **Step 3:** To make the black and orange fondant for the bats, add a small amount of food coloring gel to some fondant, then knead the color into the fondant using your hands. (Or use pre-colored fondant, available at craft stores.) Roll out the black and orange fondant separately and use cookie cutters to cut out the bat shapes. Dampen the backs of the bats with a clean, wet fingertip and press them onto the cake.

DEVILISHLY DELICIOUS TREATS

79

78

➳ 78 ➵

FOR AN EASY DESSERT, trick out frosted store-bought cupcakes (ours are topped with butter-cream frosting). First, roll out black and white fondant separately. Use cookie cutters to cut out bat and moon shapes, then let the fondant dry overnight to stiffen. Just before serving, perch the bats on the frosted cupcakes.

➳ 79 ➵

TAKE YOUR CREEPY CUPCAKES to lofty heights. Stack two or three cake pedestals on top of one another.

✦ 80 ✦

EVEN THE MOST SUPERSTITIOUS
guest will enjoy crossing paths with this black cat,
crafted from sparkling sugar. Frost two 8-inch-round
cake layers with your favorite icing, leaving as smooth
a surface as possible all over the cake. Microwave black
fondant for 8 to 10 seconds, then roll it out to ⅛-inch
thickness, and with a ruler as a guide, cut three strips
long enough to wrap around the cake's circumference;
adhere the strips around the cake, using extra dabs of
icing if needed to affix the strips. Chill the cake. Resize
the cat image on page 140 on a copier, scaling the
image to fit your cake. To create the stencil, tape the
cat image to a thin piece of cardboard, trace around
the cat, then cut the cat shape out of the cardboard.
Immediately before serving, center the cardboard
stencil on top of the cake. Fill in the stencil with black
sanding sugar, leaving the edges a little messy for a
spooky effect. Add a candy-coated sunflower seed or
a pumpkin seed for the cat's eye.

✦ 81 ✦

TIP: Roast pumpkin seeds for a special treat.
Preheat the oven to 350°F. Place 3 cups fresh pumpkin
seeds, 4 cups water, and 2 teaspoons salt in a large
saucepan and bring to a boil for 15 minutes. Drain the
seeds, blot them dry, and toss them with 1 tablespoon of
olive oil, ¼ teaspoon paprika, and 1 teaspoon salt. Spread
the seeds in a single layer on a nonstick baking pan and
roast until the seeds are golden and crisp—about 30
minutes. Makes 3 cups. Store in the freezer.

82

FASHION ITSY-BITSY SPIDERWEBS
using super-easy white-chocolate toppers that appear to float, Houdini-like, over chocolate cupcakes.

✛ **Step 1:** Download the spiderweb template at countryliving.com/oct-templates. Resize it on a copier, scaling the image to fit your cupcakes.

✛ **Step 2:** To make the webs, microwave 2 cups of white-chocolate chips in a bowl for 30 seconds and stir. Continue to microwave in 20-second intervals until almost melted. Stir again until the chocolate is completely melted. Pour the chocolate into a resealable plastic bag, seal the bag, and snip off a tiny corner to create a piping sleeve. Line a cookie sheet with parchment paper, and slide the template underneath the parchment paper.

✛ **Step 3:** To make each web, use the piping sleeve to trace white chocolate in the shape of a web, making sure to connect all the lines. Repeat the process until you've created the number of toppers you need. Chill them in the refrigerator for 10 minutes. Then, using a spatula, remove the webs carefully from the parchment paper and position one on top of each homemade or store-bought frosted cupcake.

83

TREAT GUESTS to their very own cakes with these bite-size, licorice-eared mice.

+ **Step 1:** Preheat oven to 350°F. Prepare your favorite cake batter (homemade or from a mix). Coat a mini egg-shaped cake pan with cooking spray and fill each compartment to the top with the batter. Bake the mice cakes for 15 to 20 minutes, then cool the cakes on a wire rack. Repeat until you've baked 16 cakes.

+ **Step 2:** Slowly add black food coloring to three-fourths of a tub of vanilla frosting, stirring until the frosting turns pale gray. Microwave for 10 seconds, and stir some more; repeat until the frosting is thin enough to pour, then coat the cakes with the frosting. Apply pieces of licorice to form tails (cut to 4 inches) and shaped ears (cut to 2½ inches), as shown in the photo.

+ **Step 3:** Slowly add black food coloring to the remaining frosting, while stirring, until the frosting turns dark black. Pour the frosting into a resealable plastic bag, seal the bag, and snip off a tiny corner to create a piping sleeve. Use the piping sleeve to draw eyes, noses, and whiskers on the mice.

86

THIS HUMOROUS TAKE on an X-ray is an easy way to tickle your guests' funny bones. The cake can be store-bought or homemade, and the decoration is painless to produce. The essential tool? A box of white fondant.

+ **Step 1:** Microwave the fondant for 8 to 10 seconds, then roll it out on a clean work surface to a ⅛-inch thickness. Create the control panel at the bottom of the cake by cutting a strip that's long enough to wrap around both sides of one of the cake's narrow ends; lay it in place.

+ **Step 2:** For the X-ray label, cut a small fondant rectangle and dampen one side with water, then center it on the control panel.

+ **Step 3:** Fill a resealable plastic bag with chocolate frosting, seal the bag, and snip off a tiny corner. Pipe *X-ray* on the label.

+ **Step 4:** Devise knobs by affixing white Necco wafers, then Reese's Pieces, to the panel with dabs of chocolate icing.

+ **Step 5:** Using this photo as a guide, cut fondant strips and roll them with your hands to shape skinny bones; for the spinal column, form strips into balls and flatten slightly. Transfer the bones to the cake. Next, add a hard-candy heart.

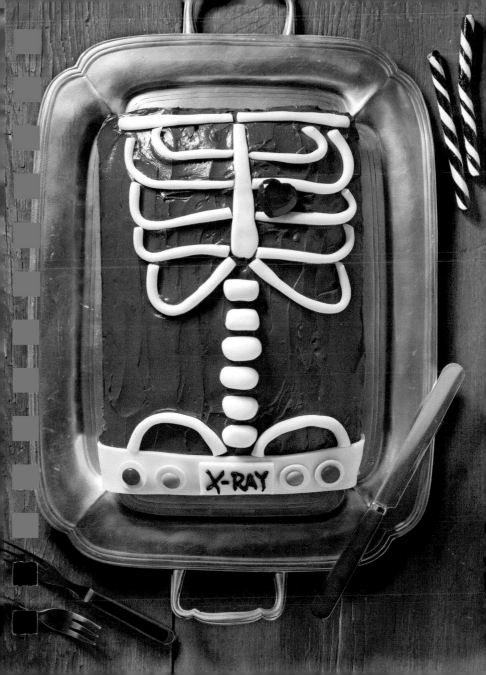

87

TURN LOLLIPOPS INTO a grave affair. To make these clever covers for candy suckers, use the tombstone image on page 135 and follow the steps below.

+ **Step 1:** For each lollipop, photocopy and cut out two tombstones, then attach them, faceup, to a sheet of black construction paper with a glue stick. When dry, cut around each tombstone, leaving a black construction-paper border, as shown.

+ **Step 2:** Turn one tombstone facedown and glide the glue stick along its outer edges at the top and sides only. Place the other tombstone on top of it, faceup. Press the edges together to create one cover. Let dry.

+ **Step 3:** Use a fine-tipped black marker to spell out *RIP*—or a guest's name—on one side.

+ **Step 4:** Repeat the directions above to create additional lollipop covers. Insert candy. Place floral foam in a bowl and stand the lollipops in the foam. Then fill the bowl with crushed chocolate cookies (we used Oreos here) to serve as the dirt in your graveyard.

➡ 88 ⬅

TREAT YOUR GUESTS to this refreshing punch, developed by Chef James Boyce. It's a tempting take on fall's favorite fruit.

APPLE CIDER PUNCH

Makes 16 servings; total time 10 minutes

1 half-gallon apple cider, chilled
1 quart white grape juice, chilled
1 (750-ml) bottle sparkling apple cider, chilled

8 ounces orange juice
16 star anises, for garnish
1 large Golden Delicious apple, sliced crosswise, for garnish
16 ounces dark rum (optional)

1. In a punch bowl or large pitcher, combine the apple cider, grape juice, sparkling cider, and orange juice.

2. To serve, fill tumblers with ice. Add one ounce of rum to each glass, if desired, and top with punch. Garnish each with an star anise and an apple slice.

➡ 89 ⬅

TIP: Give your friends a reason to bug out by cooling their drinks with "fly-infested" ice. Simply drop small raisins in an ice tray filled with water; once the cubes freeze, the dark bits of fruit take on the disturbing appearance of trapped insects.

⊷ 90 ⊶

CHOCOLATE TOPPING OOZING over orange frosting gives this bewitching cake the look of the season. To achieve this cascading layer of glaze, gently spread it over the cake's edge with the back of a spoon or an offset spatula. If more is needed, add only a little at a time.

CHOCOLATE TOPPING

Makes 1 cup

4 ounces bittersweet chocolate, chopped
1 tablespoon unsalted butter, cold

3 tablespoons corn syrup
½ cup heavy cream

1. In a medium heatproof bowl, stir together the chocolate, butter, and corn syrup.

2. In a small saucepan, bring the cream to a boil, pour it over the chocolate mixture, and let sit for 3 minutes. Gently stir, using a whisk, until smooth. Let sit for 3 to 5 minutes, until the glaze thickens slightly.

3. Pour the glaze onto the center of a homemade or store-bought frosted cake and smooth out to the edges to allow the glaze to drip over the sides.

⟞⟶ 91 ⟵⟝

SPIN A SWEET SPIDERWEB over the top of a luscious chocolate cake. All you need are a toothpick and a steady hand to make this delicate cobweb pattern. Store in a cool area.

To create the web effect, pour Chocolate Glaze over the top of an un-iced homemade or store-bought layer cake. Spread the glaze over the cake's edges and smooth the sides. Fill a small piping bag with three to four tablespoons of melted white chocolate. Starting at the center of the top of the cake, pipe the white chocolate in a spiral. Drag a toothpick from the center of the spiral to the cake's edge. Repeat every 1½ inches.

CHOCOLATE GLAZE

Makes 1½ cups

9 ounces bittersweet chocolate, finely chopped

1½ tablespoons unsalted butter

½ cup heavy cream

Place the chocolate and butter together in a medium heatproof bowl and set aside. In a small saucepan, heat the heavy cream until it just begins to boil and immediately pour over the chocolate. Stir gently until smooth. Let sit until slightly thickened before using to glaze cakes, about 3 minutes. Place the cake in the refrigerator for 5 to 10 minutes to set.

PUMPKINS' CHARMS are more than skin deep—see for yourself with this moist pumpkin bread. Try it with butter or cream cheese.

PUMPKIN BREAD

Makes 2 loaves; Total time: 1 hr. 20 min.

2 sticks unsalted butter, melted, plus more for greasing pans

2½ cups all-purpose flour, plus more for dusting pans

1 cup light-brown sugar

1 cup granulated sugar

2 teaspoons baking powder

1 teaspoon baking soda

2 teaspoons cinnamon

¾ teaspoon ground cloves

2 cups grated pumpkin (use a small-holed grate)

3 large eggs

½ cup buttermilk

1½ teaspoons vanilla extract

1. Preheat the oven to 350°F. Butter and flour two 9- by 5-inch loaf pans or two 8-inch cake pans and set aside.

2. In a large bowl, combine the flour, sugars, baking powder, baking soda, and spices. Add the grated pumpkin and toss.

3. In a medium bowl, whisk the eggs, buttermilk, butter, and vanilla, and stir into the dry ingredients.

4. Transfer to the prepared pans and bake on the middle rack of the oven until a wooden skewer inserted into the center of the bread tests clean, about 35 minutes. Cool in pans on a wire rack. Run a knife around the edges to release the bread from the pans.

93

BAT-SHAPED SUGAR COOKIES add appeal to a homemade or store-bought frosted cake.

To make the cookies, preheat the oven to 375°F. Prepare one package of sugar cookie mix per the package instructions. Once the ingredients are combined, slowly add black food coloring while mixing the dough on slow speed, until the dough turns dark black. Wrap and chill the dough for 15 minutes. On a floured surface, roll the dough to a ⅛-inch thickness and cut out cookies with bat-shaped cutters. Place the cookies on a lined baking sheet, chill for 10 minutes, then bake for 7 to 10 minutes. To make the moon, beat one 16-ounce

tub of vanilla frosting in a mixer for 15 seconds or until spreadable. Apply the frosting in crescent shape as shown in photo. Arrange a few cookies atop the moon and serve the remainder on a separate platter.

94

NO HALLOWEEN CELEBRATION would be complete without classic, hand-dipped caramel apples. Smaller apple varieties are best for young children.

CARAMEL APPLES
Makes 12

12 crisp apples
1⅓ cups dark corn syrup
1⅓ cups granulated sugar
1⅓ cups light brown sugar
1⅓ cups heavy cream

¼ teaspoon salt
3 tablespoons butter
¾ teaspoon vanilla
    extract

Line a baking pan with a generously oiled sheet of parchment paper. Push a candy apple stick into the core of each apple. Combine the syrup, sugars, heavy cream, and salt in a large saucepan over medium-high heat. Simmer until the mixture reaches 270°F on a candy thermometer—about 15 minutes. Remove from heat, stir in the butter and vanilla. Let cool for 6 to 8 minutes, until the caramel thickens to a toffeelike consistency. Dip and gently swirl the apples in the caramel and place on the prepared baking sheet. Let cool completely. To decorate, dip the caramel-covered apples in melted nonpareils, or drizzle them with melted chocolate.

95

THE MAGIC INGREDIENTS for these bewitching apples? A deep crimson variety like Red Delicious, a few drops of food coloring, plus a dash of spicy cinnamon.

DECADENTLY DARK CANDY APPLES

Makes 6–8

6–8 Red Delicious apples
3 cups sugar
½ cup light corn syrup
½ teaspoon cinnamon-flavored oil

¼ tablespoon red food coloring
¼ tablespoon black food coloring (for black apples)

1. Remove the stems and skewer the apples (see Tricks for Sticks on page 125).

2. In a saucepan over high heat, with a candy thermometer attached, heat the sugar, one cup water, and the corn syrup, stirring until the sugar dissolves. Bring to a boil until the mixture reaches 300°F. Remove from heat, and stir in the cinnamon-flavored oil and the red food coloring.

   To make red apples: Grease a baking sheet. Dip the apples, one at a time, in the red syrup, then transfer to the baking sheet. Let cool, about 10 minutes.

   To make black apples: Grease a baking sheet. Add the black food coloring to your red syrup. (If the syrup has thickened, reheat it briefly.) Dip the apples in the black syrup, one at a time, then transfer to the baking sheet. Let cool, about 10 minutes.

96

NO CAMPFIRE NEEDED: Marshmallows, chocolate, and graham crackers meet their match in a tart Granny Smith.

TRIPLE-DIPPED S'MORES APPLES

Makes 6–8

6–8 Granny Smith apples
  2 tablespoons unsalted
    butter
  1 (28-ounce) bag large
    marshmallows

10 ounces milk chocolate
  chips
About 2 cups crushed
  graham crackers,
  placed in a bowl

1. Remove the stems and skewer the apples (see Tricks for Sticks on page 125) and line a baking sheet with parchment paper.

2. In a large saucepan over low heat, warm the butter. Add the marshmallows, and stir until melted. Dip the apples, one at a time, then transfer to the parchment-lined baking sheet. Refrigerate until set, about 15 minutes.

3. Line another baking sheet with parchment paper. In a double boiler over low heat, melt the chocolate chips, stirring continuously. Dip an apple into the chocolate, stopping two-thirds of the way up. Immediately dip the lower third of the apple into the bowl of crushed graham crackers, rotating to coat evenly. Transfer to the parchment-lined baking sheet. Repeat for all the apples and refrigerate until set, about 15 minutes.

97

CLOAKED IN CREAMY WHITE CHOCOLATE
and coconut, pink Fujis become
positively pale.

GHOSTLY COCONUT-COVERED APPLES

Makes 6–8

6–8 Fuji apples
About 4 cups shredded
coconut, placed in a bowl

10 ounces white
chocolate chips

1. Remove the stems and skewer the apples (see Tricks for Sticks below). Line a baking sheet with parchment paper.

2. In a double boiler over low heat, melt the chocolate chips, stirring. Dip an apple into the chocolate. Immediately dip the apple into the bowl of shredded coconut, rotating to coat evenly. Transfer the apple to the parchment-lined baking sheet. Repeat for all the apples and refrigerate until set, about 15 minutes.

TRICKS FOR STICKS First, simply twist off the stem of the apple. If your skewer is blunt, sharpen it by using a utility knife to slice off one end at a diagonal angle. Then, working on a flat surface, firmly grip your apple and push the skewer two-thirds of the way in. If any juice leaks out, blot the fruit with a paper towel before dipping. Twigs from your yard work just fine as skewers. Use a damp paper towel to wipe them clean before inserting them into the apple.

✦ 98 ✦

RAISINS AND CHUNKS of dried fruit dot these irresistible and easy-to-make sweet and sticky treats.

SWEET POPCORN BALLS

12 cups popped popcorn
3 cups mixed dried fruit
   such as golden raisins,
   cherries, and chopped
   apricots and figs

1¼ cups granulated sugar
¾ cup brown sugar
1 cup corn syrup
½ cup water

Toss the popcorn and dried fruit together in a large, lightly oiled, heatproof bowl. Oil two waxed paper–lined baking pans and a long metal fork. Set aside. In a medium saucepan fitted with a candy thermometer, bring the granulated sugar, brown sugar, corn syrup, and water to a boil over medium-high heat. Reduce the heat to medium and cook until the mixture reaches 260°F on a candy thermometer. Carefully pour the syrup over the popcorn mixture. Stir with the fork to distribute evenly. Let the mixture sit for 1 to 2 minutes. With well-oiled hands, form 3-inch balls, place on pans, and let cool completely. Store in an airtight container for up to 4 days.

Note: Getting the sugar to the right temperature and consistency is the most important step in this recipe. To properly gauge the temperature, use a candy thermometer that can be clipped to the side of the pan. For an accurate reading, avoid letting the probe touch the bottom of the pan, and check the temperature in several spots.

Recipe variations: For a change of pace, omit the chunks of dried fruit and substitute black and orange jelly beans, roasted peanuts, or even toasted pumpkin seeds (see page 96). To please chocolate lovers, drizzle the finished popcorn balls with melted dark chocolate and let set on waxed paper.

Presentation: Once the popcorn balls have cooled and set, wrap them in orange- or black-colored cellophane and tie closed with a coordinating ribbon. Serve to guests on a plate or in a bowl to help minimize mess.

⇒ 99 ⇐

SPIN SOME DELICIOUS BLACK MAGIC and make the cake shown on page 88. Using your favorite recipe or store-bought mix, follow the baking directions through the cooling stage. Then ice the top of one cake layer with vanilla frosting and place the second cake layer on top. Ice the entire double-layered cake. Chill the iced cake in the refrigerator for 15 minutes. Resize the spider stencil on page 140, scaling the image to fit your cake. To create the stencil, tape the stencil to a thin piece of cardboard, trace around the spider, then cut the spider shape out of the cardboard and center the stencil on the cake. Sprinkle black sanding sugar to cover the image, keeping the rest of the cake clean. Press the sugar lightly with your fingers to make sure it adheres. Brush off excess sugar and carefully remove the stencil.

100

DECORATING THESE BROWNIES is eerily simple. Simply lay a swatch of lace on one of the treats. Sift confectioners' sugar over the top, then carefully remove the lace; repeat for the remaining brownies.

101

TREAT YOUR GUESTS to some sinful sweets. Frost sugar cookies with white royal icing, allowing it to set overnight. Next, put a small amount of black gel paste in a shallow dish, and lay two stacked paper towels atop the gel paste. Press a skull-and-crossbones rubber stamp onto the towels and then onto one iced cookie; repeat the process for the entire batch.

100

101

Linoleum-Tool-Carved Pumpkins (pages 12, 13, 23, 38, and 39)

Using linoleum-cutting tools to create a design on the pumpkin's surface is not only easier than carving, but it also allows the pumpkin to emit a subtle glow when illuminated. You can find sets of linoleum cutters for less than $10 at art-supply stores or on websites such as misterart.com.

+ **Step 1:** Hollow out pumpkins from the bottom for a cleaner look. Scoop out additional flesh behind the design once you've carved it, to make sure light can shine through. (Leave about ¼ to ½ inch of pumpkin flesh.)

+ **Step 2:** Sketch the design on the pumpkin with a pencil to figure out the preferred size and placement, then draw your pattern on the pumpkin with a grease pencil.

+ **Step 3:** Use a linoleum cutter to make partial cuts. Score the outline with a thin tip; scrape out larger areas with a thick tip.

+ **Step 4:** In each pumpkin, place votive candles set inside glass holders filled with a little water so the candle will go out when it burns down. Or insert a small string of battery-operated Christmas lights.

Découpage 101 (page 16)

+ **Step 1:** Cover your workspace with wax paper; then pour Mod Podge Matte all-in-one découpage sealer into a mixing bowl.

+ **Step 2:** Using a narrow foam brush, spread an even coat of Mod Podge on the back of a printed or copied image.

+ **Step 3:** Press the image onto your Funkin, smoothing out any air bubbles; repeat steps 2 and 3 for the remaining images. Tip: To make an image better fit the contours of a Funkin, you may want to cut small slits at the top and/or bottom of the paper. When covering an entire Funkin, it's also helpful to suspend the faux gourd in a bowl and work on one half at a time (let dry for about 10 minutes before flipping to complete the other side).

✛ **Step 4:** Once all the images have been applied, use a foam brush to spread a thin coat of Mod Podge on the entire Funkin. (Again, it's helpful to suspend the Funkin in a bowl and coat one half at a time; let dry for about 10 minutes before flipping to complete the other side.) Let dry for one hour, then repeat with a second coat to seal. Let dry for one full day.

Crepe-Paper Wreath (page 48)

✛ **Step 1:** Cut a four-inch-long strip of black streamer and fold it in half (you'll need upward of 100 cut-and-folded strips). Select any spot on a 14-inch foam wreath form and pin three strips side by side so they overlap to form one row. (We used straight pins with black heads.)

✛ **Step 2:** Directly beneath that first row, pin another overlapping row of three folded strips. Continue creating rows until you've gone almost all the way around the wreath form.

✛ **Step 3:** Just before you return to your starting point, loop a two-foot-long streamer over the wreath. Trim the ends to about eight inches long, then cut a decorative V into each. Fluff the folded streamers, and you're ready to display your finished wreath.

Crepe-Paper Bouquet (page 47)

✤ **Step 1:** Bend an 18-inch-long piece of floral wire in half and wrap double-sided tape around the bent end about five times.

✤ **Step 2:** Hold the tip of a streamer, still attached to its roll, against the top of the taped wire. Then loosely wrap it around the wire four times to create an inner bud, pinching the bottom edge of the streamer against the taped wire as you go.

✤ **Step 3:** Continue wrapping the streamer around the wire, gathering the paper at the flower's base so that the petals fan out at the top. Continue until you have a full flower. Finish by cutting and securing the flower to the wire with floral tape. Repeat until you have enough blooms to fill a bowl.

Friendly Ghosts (page 72)

To set up a workstation, stack one small paper cup atop another that's turned upside down. (For extra stability, tape the cups together.) Inflate a small balloon and rest it in the top cup. Cut cheesecloth into pieces that measure about eight inches square and fill a bowl with fabric stiffener.

✢ **Step 1:** Soak a piece of cheesecloth in fabric stiffener and immediately drape it over the balloon. Let dry for 10 minutes.

✢ **Step 2:** Pop the balloon with a pin to reveal a hardened shape. Cut two tiny circles out of black felt for eyes and affix them to the ghost with tacky glue.

✢ **Step 3:** Remove the ghost from the cup and use your fingers to rough up the ends of the cheesecloth. Thread fishing line through the top of each ghost, securing with a knot to hang.

place on fold

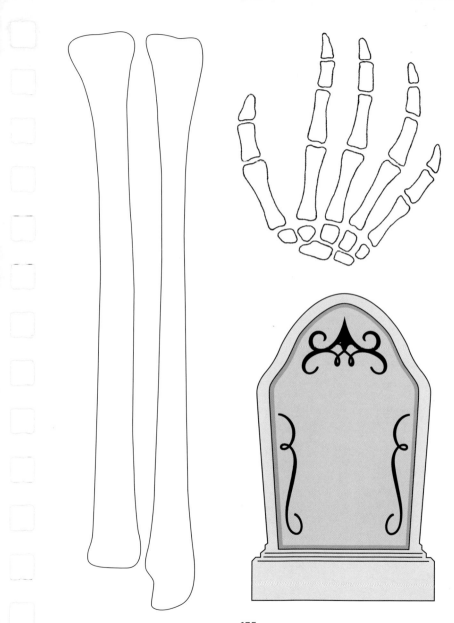

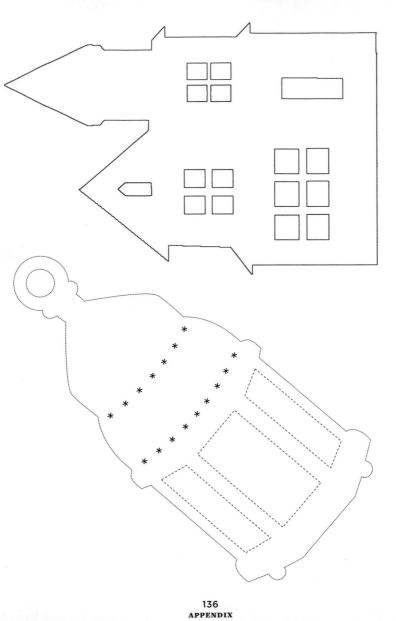

apply bead of glue along here

apply glue here   and here

139

Sang An: 79, 80

Matt Armendariz: 121, 123, 124

Burcu Avsar: 22, 31, 32, 62, 73

Quentin Bacon: 33, 42, 74, 129

Matthew Benson: 36

Susie Cushner: 63

Dana Gallagher: 8, 14, 17, 28, 70, 75

Dane Holweger: 71

John Kernick: 2, 6, 11, 18, 21 bottom, 25, 35, 37, 41, 45, 47, 48, 49, 57, 77, 78, 85, 86, 87, 90 top, 93, 94

David A. Land: 53

Keith Scott Morton: 58

Laura Moss: 72, 109

Marcus Nilsson: 117

Kana Okada: 110

Con Poulos: 88, 99, 101, 118

Steven Randazzo: 12, 13, 23, 38, 39

Hector Sanchez: 102, 105, 107

Charles Schiller: 90 bottom, 97, 113, 114

Seth Smoot: 46, 54, 55, 60 top, 66 top

Studio D: Philip Friedman: 52, 65, 69, 82, 132 (all photos), 133 (all photos); Lara Robby: 131 (all photos)

Mikkel Vang: 50, 59, 60 bottom, 66 bottom, 76

Björn Wallander: 21 top

Index